TIME TRAVEL GUIDES

MEDIEVAL
EUROPE

John Haywood

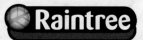
Raintree

www.raintree.co.uk/library
Visit our website to find out more information about Raintree books.

To order:
☎ Phone 44 (0) 1865 888112
🖹 Send a fax to 44 (0) 1865 314091
💻 Visit the Raintree bookshop at www.raintree.co.uk/library to browse our catalogue and order online.

First published in Great Britain by Raintree, Halley Court, Jordan Hill, Oxford OX2 8EJ, part of Pearson Education. Raintree is a registered trademark of Pearson Education Ltd.

© Pearson Education Ltd 2008
First published in paperback 2008
The moral right of the proprietor has been asserted.

ISBN 978-1-406-20996-9 (hardback)
12 11 10 09 08
10 9 8 7 6 5 4 3 2 1

ISBN 978-1-406-21001-9 (paperback)
12 11 10 09 08
10 9 8 7 6 5 4 3 2 1

British Library Cataloguing-in-Publication Data
Haywood, John, 1956-
  Medieval Europe. - (Time travel guides)
  1. Civilization, Medieval - Juvenile literature
  940.1
A full catalogue record for this book is available from the British Library.

This levelled text is a version of *Freestyle: Time Travel Guides: Medieval Europe.*

Acknowledgements
The publishers would like to thank the following for permission to reproduce photographs (t = top, b= bottom):
AKG pp. **11** (b) (British Library), **14** (British Library), **17** (British Library), **18** (Bibliothèque Nationale, Paris), **30** (Herve Champollion), **31**, **36** (British Library), **40** (British Library), **45** (British Library), **47** (Bibliothèque Nationale, Paris), **48/49** (Jost Schilgen); Art Archive pp. **26** (Palazzo Pubblico, Siena /Dagli Orti), **34** (Musée Condé Chantilly/ Dagli Orti), **37** (Corbis/Alfredo Dagli Orti), **53** (Bibliothèque Municipale, Moulins/Dagli Orti); Bridgeman Art Library pp. **8** (Musée de l'Oeuvre de Nôtre Dame, Strasbourg, France/Giraudon), **11** (t) (Biblioteca Monasterio del Escorial, Madrid, Spain/Giraudon), **15** (Rheinisches Landesmuseum, Bonn, Germany/Giraudon), **19** (Museum of London, UK), **21** (Bibliothèque Municipale, Cambrai, France/Giraudon), **23** (Museum of London, UK), **38** (Palazzo Pubblico, Siena, Italy/ Alinari), **41** (Osterreichische Nationalbibliothek, Vienna, Austria/Alinari), **42** (Musée de la Tapisserie, Bayeux, France/With special authorization of the city of Bayeux/ Giraudon), **44** (Osterreichische Nationalbibliothek, Vienna, Austria/Alinari), **51** (Bibliothèque Nationale, Paris, France/Archives Charmet), **52** (Glasgow University Library, Scotland); Corbis pp. **6/7** (Michael Busselle), **12** (Patrick Ward), **28** (Karl-Josef Hildenbrand/dpa), **54/55** (Elio Ciol); John Haywood pp. **24/25**.

Cover photographs of (1) Arundel Castle, Arundel, West Sussex, England reproduced with permission of Adam van Bunnens /Alamy; (2) Super Decretales Manuscript (ca. 1300–1399) courtesy of Museum of Biblioteca Capitular Tortosa/Ramon Manent/Corbis; (3) a 13th-century ivory carving of a knight from a chess set courtesy of The Art Archive/Corbis.

The publishers would like to thank Dr. Susan Edgington for her assistance in the preparation of this book.

Every effort has been made to contact copyright holders of any material reproduced in this book. Any omissions will be rectified in subsequent printings if notice is given to the publishers.

CONTENTS

Words that appear in the text in bold, **like this**, are explained in the glossary.

Legend

- Pilgrimage destinations
- Universities

ATLANTIC OCEAN

KINGDOM OF NORWAY

KINGDOM OF SCOTLAND

IRELAND

KINGDOM OF DENMARK

KINGDOM OF ENGLAND

Oxford
London
Canterbury

Nôtre Dame

PRINCIPALITY OF WALES

Pilgrim cross

NORMANDY
Paris

Santiago de Compostela

KINGDOM OF FRANCE

HOLY ROMAN EMPIRE

KINGDOM OF NAVARRE

Bologna

Rome

KINGDOM OF LEON

KINGDOM OF PORTUGAL

KINGDOM OF CASTILE

KINGDOM OF ARAGON

MUSLIM STATES

MEDITERRANEAN SEA

FINNS

KINGDOM
OF SWEDEN

BALTS

RUSSIAN
PRINCIPALITIES

N

W E

S

POLAND

MAP OF MEDIEVAL EUROPE, AROUND AD 1200

KINGDOM
OF
HUNGARY

BLACK SEA

BYZANTINE EMPIRE

● Constantinople
(Istanbul)

KINGDOM
OF
SICILY

These are the city walls of Avila in Spain. Avila needs these strong walls to protect itself against attack.

CHAPTER 1

FACTS ABOUT MEDIEVAL EUROPE

Do you want to see great castles and churches before they fall into ruins? Do you want to see knights in armour? If you do, then medieval Europe is the place for you.

Enjoy all the fun of a fair. Watch knights on horseback in a fighting contest. But take care. Violent crime is common in medieval Europe. Disease is everywhere.

WHEN TO TRAVEL

The medieval period is the time between the late 5th century AD and the mid-15th century. That's between about 1,530 and 550 years ago.

THE EARLY MEDIEVAL PERIOD

The medieval period started when the **Roman Empire** ended. The Roman Empire was the group of countries ruled by ancient Rome. It ended after Germanic tribes forced their way into the lands. Germanic tribes were people from the north and east of Europe.

When this happened, Europe was thrown into chaos. Wars were breaking out everywhere.

This stained glass window shows the Emperor Charlemagne. About 1,200 years ago, Charlemagne ruled most of western Europe.

MEDIEVAL EUROPE AT ITS HEIGHT

By the early 1100s (about 900 years ago), things are improving in western Europe. There are new kingdoms with strong rulers. New schools and universities are opening. Great cathedrals and castles are being built.

THE END OF THE MEDIEVAL PERIOD

After 1300, medieval Europe is not a good place to be. Wars and disease cause great suffering. There is also **famine**. Famine is when people starve because of a food shortage.

In the 1400s, the way of life begins to change. The medieval period ends.

THE BLACK DEATH!

The **Black Death** is a horrible disease. It sweeps through Europe between 1346 and 1351. There is no cure. If you catch it, you will probably die.

GOOD AND BAD TIMES TO VISIT

793–911	The worst period for **Viking** pirate attacks on western Europe. Vikings are bands of people from northern Europe.
1066–1070	England is being **conquered** (taken over) by the Normans from northern France (see map on page 4). This is a bad time to visit.
1096–1099	European armies conquer the **Holy Land**. The Holy Land is modern-day Israel and Palestine.
1100–1300	Medieval Europe reaches its peak.
1337–1453	England and France fight the terrible Hundred Years War.
1346–1351	The Black Death kills about 25 million people in Europe.

Key:

Stay away	Interesting times to visit	Best times to visit

CLIMATE AND LANDSCAPE

The Atlantic coasts have cool summers and mild winters (see map on pages 4–5). Central and eastern Europe gets hot summers but freezing winters. The hottest weather is around the Mediterranean.

FORESTS AND WILDLIFE

Forests in lowland areas have been cut down long ago. This has made way for fields and villages. The remaining woods provide people with firewood and timber. You still find bears and wolves in the thick mountain forests.

FARMLANDS

Most medieval Europeans are farmers. They live in small cottages. These are grouped around a church and a **manor** house. The manor house is where the lord of the village and farmlands lives.

DRAGON TALES

Stories about dragons are popular in medieval Europe. People believe that dragons are dangerous creatures that live in caves. Luckily, they do not really exist.

This picture shows a farmer ploughing a field. Oxen (male cattle) are pulling the plough. The farmer's wife is scattering seeds for next year's crops.

Village farmlands are divided into three great fields. Crops are grown in two of the fields. Each year a different field is left **fallow**. Fallow means that no crops are grown in it. This gives the soil time to get back its goodness.

WATERMILLS AND WINDMILLS

There are lots of watermills and windmills in the countryside. These structures use the power of water or wind to run machines. Some are used for making flour or pumping water.

THE CHURCH

The Church is very important in medieval Europe. The largest buildings are usually churches. Almost everyone you meet will be a Christian. Christians follow the teachings of Jesus Christ. Medieval Europeans believe that other religions are false.

This huge cathedral is in the city of York in England. It was built between the 13th and 15th centuries. That's between 800 and 600 years ago.

PATRON SAINTS

Patron saints are believed to protect places or people. Some protect animals and specific activities. Here are some well-known patron saints of medieval times.

St Christopher: patron saint of travellers. He is believed to have carried the boy Jesus across a deep river.

St Francis: patron saint of animals. This is because he loved nature and wildlife.

St Joseph: patron saint of carpenters. St Joseph worked as a carpenter.

St Lawrence: patron saint of cooks. This is because he was roasted alive!

St Nicholas: patron saint of children. In modern times St Nicholas is better known as Santa Claus.

St Olaf: patron saint of the country of Norway. Olaf was a Norwegian king. He worked to bring Christianity to Norway.

RULERS OF THE CHURCH

The ruler of the Church in western Europe is the **pope**. The pope is chosen by senior churchmen called cardinals. Cardinals give advice to the pope.

GOING TO CHURCH

Going to church on Sundays is an important occasion. People always dress in their best clothes. Church services are in **Latin**. This is the language of ancient Rome. Most churchgoers don't understand it.

NOBLES, KNIGHTS, AND SERFS

People in medieval Europe are divided into different **ranks**, or levels. At the top are the kings and queens. Then come the nobles. Nobles are wealthy lords.

Priests and **merchants** are in the middle. Merchants are people who buy and sell goods. **Craftsmen** also belong to the middle ranks. They are people skilled at making things. At the bottom are people called **serfs**. Serfs are poor farmers.

This picture shows three types of medieval people. It shows a priest (left), a knight (centre), and a farmer (right).

BARONS AND KNIGHTS

The highest nobles are the **barons**. They have titles such as duke or count. Barons live in castles. They rule an area for the king. In wartime they must provide **knights** for the king's army.

Knights are the lowest nobles. They fight on horseback in the king's army. Most knights live in **manor** houses (see page 10).

SERFS

Serfs live on land owned by a lord. A serf must give his lord one-third of all the crops he grows. He must also give one-tenth to the Church.

Serfs usually live in small cottages. They need their lord's permission to leave the village. They also need his permission to marry.

This picture shows serfs gathering wheat. ↘

THE KINGDOMS OF EUROPE

Most countries in medieval Europe are ruled by kings. The most powerful countries are France, England, and the **Holy Roman Empire**.

ENGLAND

England is one of Europe's best-ruled countries. This is because of its strong rulers. William the Conqueror took control of England in 1066 (nearly 950 years ago). William was from Normandy in France.

FRANCE

France is the most important country in medieval Europe. At one time the French king could not control the nobles. The king of England often ruled large parts of France.

This changed under the rule of Philip Augustus. Philip defeated England and the Holy Roman Empire in 1204. This was more than 800 years ago. It made France the most powerful kingdom in Europe.

THE HUNDRED YEARS WAR

Avoid France during the terrible Hundred Years War with England (1337–1453). War began when Edward III of England claimed he should be king of France. In the end, England was defeated.

This picture shows King Philip Augustus of France. He is talking to a **bishop**. A bishop is a senior priest.

THE HOLY ROMAN EMPIRE

The Holy Roman Empire was created by the German king Otto I. Otto ruled from 936 to 973 (more than 1,000 years ago). He took control of a large area of Europe. Otto and later Holy Roman emperors have problems controlling parts of the empire.

OTHER IMPORTANT RULERS

Charlemagne, king of the Franks (ruled 769–814)

Alfred the Great, king of the English (ruled 871–899)

Frederick Barbarossa, Holy Roman emperor (ruled 1152–1190)

Louis IX, king of France (ruled 1226–1270)

Edward I, king of England (ruled 1272–1307)

FEUDALISM AND CHIVALRY

Feudalism plays an important part in medieval life. So does **chivalry**. Feudalism is the system in which a **knight** (warrior) serves a king or lord. Chivalry is how a knight should behave.

FEUDALISM

Feudalism is a way for kings and lords to keep armies of knights. It takes 14 years of training to become a knight. It also takes a lot of money. To afford this, a knight must serve a rich lord or king.

OATHS

This painting shows a knight making an oath. An oath is a promise made before other people and a holy object. Oaths are used in important agreements. Breaking an oath is a serious crime.

The knight must promise to fight for his lord. In return, the lord gives the knight land and property. The knight loses this if he fails to support his lord.

CHIVALRY

Chivalry is how knights are expected to behave. It is also about the qualities they should have.

A chivalrous knight rides and fights well. He is a good Christian. He should protect the weak and treat women politely. Sadly, not all knights follow the rules of chivalry.

This is a charter signed by King John of England (1199–1216). A charter is a legal document from a ruler. It gives or explains the rights of his people. The ruler must keep to the rules written in the document.

MEDIEVAL EDUCATION

In medieval Europe, education is run by the Church. There are cathedral schools and universities. These are mainly to educate boys who wish to become priests. But going to university can also help people to become lawyers or doctors.

MEDIEVAL UNIVERSITIES

In the late 1100s, European universities are lively places to be. New ideas are causing lots of excitement. They are also causing plenty of arguments.

Most university students are between 14 and 18 years old. Students are known for getting drunk and chasing girls. Fights between students and townspeople are common.

AN UNFAIR SYSTEM

You'll have to pay for your lessons in medieval Europe. Poor people cannot afford this. This is why most cannot read or write.

Only boys can go to school and university. Girls from noble families are sometimes taught at home.

This is a late medieval picture from France. it shows a university teacher giving a talk to students.

THE MEDIEVAL CURRICULUM

Students at a medieval university are taught ways of thinking. They learn to explain their thoughts properly. Students study arithmetic and geometry. They also learn music and astronomy. Astronomy is the study of the moon, planets, and stars.

WHAT TO WEAR

If you visit between 1100 and 1300 (between 900 and 700 years ago) you should take a tunic. Women wear long, close-fitting tunics. These reach down to the ground. Married women cover their hair in public. They may wear a hat or veil.

Men's tunics are shorter and looser than the women's. They reach to the calves. Children dress the same as the grown-ups.

RICH AND POOR

The rich wear clothes made of linen and silk. They also wear satin, velvet, and fur.

Ordinary people try to copy the way the rich dress. But they can usually only afford woollen cloth.

veil

circlet

long tunic

girdle

This is a picture of a well-to-do European woman. It shows how she would dress in the 12th century. That is about 900 years ago.

MAKING A POINT

Shoes with pointed toes are worn by men and women in medieval times. These leather shoes are from the 13th and 14th centuries. They are between 800 and 700 years old.

HAIRSTYLES

Men are usually clean-shaven and have shoulder-length hair. Women and girls have long hair. Women wear their hair in plaits or braids.

STAY OUT OF THE SUN!

Rich women take great care to protect their skin from the Sun. They like to have white skin. This shows that they do not have to work outside for a living.

This is Melrose Abbey in Scotland. It is built in the medieval style known as Gothic (see pages 28–29).

CHAPTER 2

WHERE TO GO AND WHAT TO DO

There are plenty of things to do and see in medieval Europe. Visitors are welcome at the great cathedrals and castles. Plays and **tournaments** (fighting contests) are free. You can have great fun shopping at a fair. Or you can look around the many shops in a busy town. Remember that medieval towns are not the cleanest places. Watch where you put your feet!

This is a late medieval painting of the Italian city of Siena. The streets are full of people shopping and meeting friends.

MEDIEVAL TOWNS

Many people in the country are **serfs**. They are poor people who have to obey a lord. But town people are free. They can travel and work where they wish.

The bad side of living in medieval towns is that they are dirty and smelly. They are also full of rats. Diseases can quickly spread.

SIGHTSEEING

You'll probably want to visit the cathedral first. This is usually the biggest building in a town. Large towns often have other beautiful churches too. They may also have palaces and market halls to visit.

The outdoor markets are great for shopping. They're also good for take-away food. You might want to finish your day with a visit to a public bathhouse. Medieval people do take baths, but not very often!

GUILDS

The most powerful organizations (groups) in towns are the **guilds**. These are set up by traders and **craftsmen** (skilled workers). Each craft or trade has its own guild. The guild controls the quality of training and products.

Some parents pay a guild member to train one of their sons. A boy who is being trained is called an **apprentice**. His training will last 7 years.

ARCHITECTURE

Church buildings in medieval Europe are built in one of two styles. These are the Romanesque and Gothic styles. Romanesque is fashionable from around 800 to 1150. That is between 850 and 1,200 years ago. After that the Gothic style takes over.

This is St Kilian Cathedral in Germany. It was completed in 1188. That's 820 years ago. The cathedral is built in the Romanesque style.

SOME GREAT CATHEDRALS TO VISIT

Place	Date begun	Style
Pisa, Italy	1063	Romanesque
Santiago de Compostela, Spain	1075	Romanesque
Durham, England	1093	Romanesque
Canterbury, England	1175	Gothic
Chartres, France	1194	Gothic
Cologne, Germany	1248	Gothic

ROMANESQUE ARCHITECTURE

Romanesque buildings look heavy and solid. They have very thick pillars and walls. These support heavy arched roofs. All arches and windows have round tops.

GOTHIC ARCHITECTURE

You can recognize a Gothic building (see page 24) by its pointed arches. Gothic buildings are taller and more graceful than Romanesque ones. They have large windows and high ceilings.

INSIDE A MEDIEVAL CHURCH

Medieval churches and cathedrals are richly decorated inside. The windows are filled with coloured glass. The walls are covered with religious paintings.

VISITING A MONASTERY

Monks are men who live religious lives. They live together in buildings called **monasteries**. Rich people make gifts of land and money to monasteries. This has made some monasteries very wealthy.

A MONK'S LIFE

Monks spend a lot of time praying and studying the Bible. But they must also work. They work either on the monastery's lands or by copying books.

A monastery is led by an abbot. Monks must always obey their abbot. They cannot own personal belongings or get married.

These covered walkways are known as cloisters. You will find cloisters in most medieval monasteries.

VISITING ARRANGEMENTS

All monasteries have guest rooms. Churchmen can stay for free. So can people making journeys to holy places. Other visitors may have to pay.

This picture shows monks singing at a church service.

NUNS

Women who live religious lives are called nuns. They live together in nunneries. Because they are women, people think nuns are less important than monks. Nunneries get fewer gifts than monasteries. This is why they are usually smaller and poorer.

FRIARS

Friars are men who live a religious life. Unlike monks, they do not live in monasteries. They spend their time among ordinary people. They live by begging for food and money.

CASTLES

Castles are first built in Europe in the 10th century. That is between 1,100 and 1,000 years ago. A castle is an especially strong building. It is designed to keep out attackers. But it is also the home of a **baron** or high-ranking lord. It is the centre for local rule.

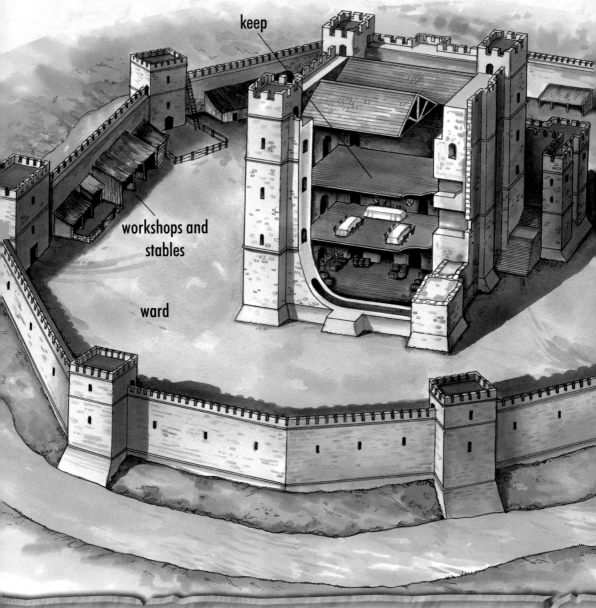

keep

workshops and stables

ward

VISITING ARRANGEMENTS

Castles are designed to keep people out in wartime. But in peacetime people need to visit. Soldiers and servants come and go. People come there to do business. Visitors are usually welcomed.

CASTLE DEFENCES

Some castles are are surrounded by a moat. A moat is a wide ditch filled with water. It makes it harder for enemies to get in. Moats are crossed by a drawbridge. This is a bridge that can be lifted up in wartime.

gatehouse

drawbridge

moat

This drawing shows the different parts of a medieval castle. The keep contains the living quarters.

ENTERTAINMENT

There is plenty of entertainment in medieval Europe. You can watch a play or go to a dance. Or you might like to listen to a **minstrel** singing. A minstrel is a travelling musician.

THRILLS AND SPILLS

Tournaments are exciting fighting contests. A tournament begins with a **joust**. This is when two **knights** (warriors) on horseback charge at one another. Each knight tries to knock the other off his horse. He does this with a long pole called a lance.

This picture is from France. It shows ladies watching knights jousting at a tournament.

The main part of the tournament is a battle between two groups of knights. This is called the mêlée. It can get very rough. The swords and spears used are not sharp. But people still get injured. They sometimes die.

THE SPORT OF KINGS

Nobles enjoy hunting on horseback. They often hunt deer and wild boar (a type of pig). Hunting without permission is a crime. It is known as poaching. Poachers are very harshly punished.

MYSTERY PLAYS

Medieval plays are either mystery plays or morality plays. Mystery plays are based on Bible stories. Morality plays are about the battle between good and evil.

All the local people get involved in putting on these plays. Even the audiences get involved in the action. There are lots of colourful costumes and music. The plays often use humour to get the message across. So they can be very funny.

SHOPPING

Medieval Europe is great for shopping. Shops are open from dawn until nightfall. You'll find shops selling similar goods grouped together in the same street.

An outdoor market is held once a week. People from the countryside come to town for this. They come to sell farm produce. They also come to buy goods such as cloth and pottery.

FUN AT THE FAIR

The fair is the biggest shopping event. It takes place once a year and lasts several days. People come from all over Europe to sell goods. They sell things such as cloth, food, and spices. Travelling entertainers add to the fun.

tapestry

This picture shows Italian **craftsmen** at work. They are making tapestries on wooden frames.

WHAT TO BUY

- **Aquamanile**: These are bronze jugs made in the shape of a knight on horseback.
- **Chess set**: Chess is a popular game in medieval times. You can buy some beautiful chess sets.
- **Souvenir badges**: These are sold at all important holy places. They are usually made of metal.

This chess piece is about 800 years old. It is made of ivory. Ivory comes from the tusks of creatures such as walruses or elephants.

MEDIEVAL MONEY

The most common medieval coin is the silver denier or penny. People make small change by cutting pennies into halves and quarters. Wherever you go, the value of a silver coin is measured by its weight.

This picture shows Pope Alexander III on horseback (centre). Walking at his side is the Holy Roman Emperor Frederick Barbarossa.

CHAPTER 3

ON THE MOVE

Travel in medieval Europe can be slow and uncomfortable. It's best to travel in short stages. Then you have the chance to meet other travellers. They may have great tales to tell.

There are plenty of places for travellers to stay. You might even be invited to spend a night in a castle. But take care. Not everyone you meet on the road will be friendly.

ROADS AND WATERWAYS

Summer is the best time to travel in medieval Europe. There are fewer storms if you are travelling by sea. Also the roads are usually dry. Wet weather makes them horribly muddy.

ON THE ROAD

The fastest way to travel overland is by horse. Buying a horse costs a lot of money. It is possible to hire one instead. If you have more money, you could travel in a carriage. Then you can expect a bumpy ride.

Most travellers have to walk. You will see lots of carts pulled by horses or oxen. But these are only used for carrying goods.

This picture shows a two-wheeled cart pulled by horses. It was painted in 1340. That's almost 670 years ago.

OVER THE SEA

In early medieval times, most ships are big open boats. In bad weather you will get wet and cold.

Later on, some ships have wooden towers at each end. Travelling by sea is still far from comfortable. But at least there is some shelter.

This picture shows a high wind at sea. At the bottom are two trade ships. They are for carrying goods. The ship in the background is a warship.

FOOD AND DRINK

RICH AND POOR

If you don't have much money, expect to eat the same foods at each meal. You will have bread and butter. You will also have cheese or gruel. Gruel is a type of very thick soup. It is made with barley and vegetables.

If you have more money, you can afford to eat other types of food. You can have lots of meat or fish. You can have pies and sweet desserts.

This is part of the Bayeux tapestry. It was made some time in the 11th century. That's more than 900 years ago. Here a bishop is blessing the food at the start of a feast.

SPICE OF LIFE

Medieval people like food with strong flavours. Many people use home-grown herbs. These include thyme, mustard, and garlic.

Spices such as pepper and ginger are also popular in cooking. But these have to be brought from distant countries. This makes them expensive.

DON'T DRINK THE WATER

It's hard to find safe drinking water in medieval Europe. In northern Europe everyone drinks beer instead. They drink about 4 litres (1 gallon) of it every day.

People in southern Europe usually drink wine. Luckily, medieval beer and wine are both low in alcohol.

WHERE TO STAY

Medieval Europe has plenty of places for travellers to stay. Towns have lots of inns. Many houses will offer bed and breakfast. Many **monasteries** (see page 30) provide comfortable guest rooms.

ROOM AT THE INN

Inns have stables for travellers' horses. Guest rooms are above the stables. Inns provide meals and drinks. They may provide entertainment too.

This Italian painting shows a thirsty traveller arriving at an inn. He is being offered a drink.

IN AN EMERGENCY

Monasteries have a duty to give free food to the poor. It is useful to know this if you are out of money. Castle kitchens have plenty of leftovers to give away too.

This is a medieval kitchen scene. A cook is preparing meat. Servants are carrying dishes out to the hall for the guests.

LIVING IT UP

Don't be afraid to ask if you can stay at a castle. Rich people often like having guests. Best of all, you won't have to pay. Don't expect luxury though. Castles can be cold and draughty.

Dinner will be held in the great hall. You will eat and drink well. There may be singers and musicians to make music while you eat.

After dinner you can go to bed. This will be on the floor of the hall with everybody else. The floor will be covered with mats or straw.

BEAT THE BUGS

You will sometimes wake up covered with little red bite marks. That grubby straw-filled mattress was full of bedbugs! Bunches of mint can help keep the bedbugs away.

PILGRIMAGE

Many travellers you meet will be on a **pilgrimage**. A pilgrimage is a long journey to a holy place. People who make these journeys are known as **pilgrims**.

People hope that making a pilgrimage will help them get into Heaven. Some hope to be cured of a disease. Others go to earn forgiveness for the bad things they have done.

TOP PILGRIMAGE DESTINATIONS

Canterbury, England – Pilgrims visit the tomb of St Thomas Beckett.

Santiago de Compostela, Spain – Pilgrims visit the tomb of St James.

Rome, Italy – This is the headquarters of the **pope** (the head of the western church).

The Holy Land – This is the land where Jesus lived and died. It is the most dangerous place to visit.

ON THE ROAD

Pilgrims often travel in groups. This for safety and company. Short pilgrimages have a holiday feel about them. But a long pilgrimage can mean many months of difficult living.

THE CRUSADES

A **crusade** is the name for a holy war. Crusaders see themselves as pilgrims with weapons. They believe they are fighting to protect the Christian religion.

The first crusade is called in 1095. It sets out to capture the city of Jerusalem in the **Holy Land**. This is the area connected with events in the Christian Bible. Jerusalem is ruled by Muslims. Muslims follow the religion of Islam.

Seven more crusades follow. In 1291 Muslims drive the crusaders out of the Holy Land for good.

This painting shows crusaders being defeated by Muslims in Jerusalem.

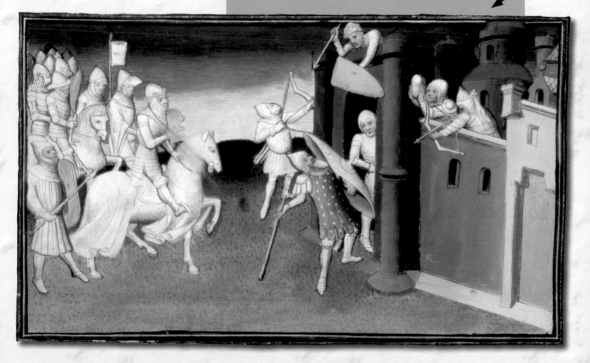

This is the Heiliggeist Hospital in the German city of Nuremberg. The hospital dates from 1331 (almost 680 years ago).

CHAPTER 4

LOOKING AFTER YOURSELF

Don't travel alone in medieval Europe. Lone travellers are easy to rob. Also you may fall ill. If this happens, it's good to have a friend to look after you. It will be hard to protect yourself from disease. This is because medieval people don't really know what causes diseases.

Be careful not to commit any crimes on your visit. Medieval punishments can be truly horrible.

DISEASE AND MEDICAL CARE

Disease is the biggest danger for medieval travellers. Dirty conditions are the main cause of disease. Unfortunately, visiting a doctor usually makes things worse. It's better to find someone who makes herbal cures. At least these are unlikely to harm you.

A STRANGE APPROACH TO MEDICINE

Medieval doctors believe that the human body is made up of four substances. These are called **humours**. Doctors think that an ill person has too much or too little of one humour.

Blood is one of the four humours. Doctors think that someone with a fever has too much blood. They may cut open a vein to remove some blood. Sometimes they use leeches. These are blood-sucking worms. Doctors don't yet realize that losing blood just weakens the patient.

DENTAL TREATMENT
If you get toothache, you will need to find a barber. He will pull out the aching tooth. But there are no drugs to stop the pain.

This picture shows a doctor visiting a patient. It also shows the patient's wife buying medicine.

HOSPITALS

Most medieval towns have at least one hospital. Hospitals are run by the Church. They just provide nursing care and try to comfort the dying. Patients often have to share beds.

LIFE EXPECTANCY

You won't see many elderly people in medieval Europe. Only 5 per cent of people live to their seventies. Only half of all children live to become adults.

CRIME AND PUNISHMENT

Violent crime seems common in medieval Europe. It is difficult to keep your belongings and money safe.

LAW ENFORCEMENT

There are no police forces. In England, crimes are looked into by officers called county sheriffs. Punishment usually means having to pay a sum of money. Murderers and people caught stealing are hanged.

Going to prison is not usually used as a punishment. Prisons are used mainly for holding people before they go on trial or to be executed.

Medieval prisons are uncomfortable and dirty. Most people are held there before being executed. ➤

Hanging is the most common form of execution. Nobles are allowed a quicker death. They may have their heads cut off instead. ➚

RELIGIOUS CRIME

In medieval Europe it is a crime to disagree with what the Church teaches. This crime is known as **heresy**. In France, Spain, and Italy there is a group to deal with it. This is called the **Holy Inquisition**.

Anyone thought guilty of heresy can be handed over to the group for questioning. The Inquisition can use torture if it thinks someone is not telling the truth. Torture causes great pain.

These stone angels and saints decorate the medieval cathedral of Notre Dame in the country of France.

CHAPTER 5

USEFUL INFORMATION

This last section contains helpful information for the time traveller. It gives you some history of the period. You will enjoy your visit more if you know a bit of history. This section also tells you about the languages that medieval people speak. Knowing something about languages can help you make friends.

LANGUAGE

The most useful language to learn before your visit is **Latin**. This is the language of the ancient Romans. Medieval people no longer speak Latin as an everyday language. But it is still used as the language of the Church and government.

Educated people understand Latin. This makes it easy for them to travel around Europe. Even the smallest village has a priest who knows Latin.

NATIONAL LANGUAGES

The languages in modern-day Europe developed in medieval times. Most languages in western Europe belong to one of two groups.

Romance languages form one group. These languages developed from local forms of Latin. French and Italian are Romance languages. So is Spanish.

The second group developed from languages spoken by ancient Germanic tribes. These were people from northern and eastern Europe. German and English belong to this group of languages. So do Swedish and Dutch.

MEDIEVAL ENGLISH

Medieval English sounds very different to modern English. It's not hard to work out the meaning of the words. But it may take a while to get used to the language. Medieval people will probably think you talk a bit strangely too.

USEFUL MEDIEVAL ENGLISH WORDS

Modern English	Medieval English	Latin
food	fode	cibus
water	water	aqua
bread	breed	panis
milk	melk	lac
soup	potage	ius
father	fader	pater
mother	moder	mater
daughter	doghter	filia
son	sone	filius

HOW DO WE KNOW ABOUT MEDIEVAL EUROPE?

We know a lot about life in medieval Europe. Medieval buildings tell us what living conditions were like. Medieval art shows us scenes of everyday life.

Some of the most important information comes from documents, books, and other written works of the time. These are usually written in **Latin** (see page 56).

CHRONICLES

Chronicles are records of events. These events were recorded in the order that they happened. Most chronicles were written by monks.

LETTERS

Medieval people who could read and write kept in touch by letter. Their letters often give details of people's private lives. They help us understand what it felt like to live in medieval times.

CHIVALRIC TALES

Stories about knights doing brave deeds were very popular in medieval times. These tales may not tell us much about how knights really behaved. But they do tell us how people thought knights should behave.

CHARTERS

Charters (see page 19) are documents from the king. They give or explain lawful rights. For example, a charter may be about the right of a town to hold a market. It may be to confirm a gift of land.

POEMS

Poems were written about all types of medieval people. Geoffrey Chaucer wrote the *Canterbury Tales* in about 1387. This long poem is about a group of **pilgrims**. They are people making a journey to a holy place in Canterbury, England. It paints an amusing picture of life in medieval England.

THE DOMESDAY BOOK

The *Domesday Book* is a record of who owned land in England. It was written in 1086. That is about 920 years ago. The Domesday Book tells us how people lived in each village. It tells us how much land they owned.

MEDIEVAL EUROPE AT A GLANCE

TIMELINE

Around 476   The western **Roman Empire** ends. The Roman Empire was the name for lands ruled by ancient Rome.

793   **Vikings** (people from Norway and Denmark) begin attacks on England.

Around 800   Most of western Europe is united under Charlemagne, king of the Franks.

886   The English king Alfred the Great defeats the Vikings.

962   The German king Otto I forms the **Holy Roman Empire**.

1066   William the Conqueror takes control of England. William comes from Normandy in northern France.

1337   The Hundred Years War between England and France begins.

1346–51   The disease known as the **Black Death** kills millions of people in Europe.

1453   The Hundred Years War ends in defeat for England.

RELIGION

Around 1000   **Pilgrimages** become popular. These are long journeys to holy places.

1095   Pope Urban II calls a **crusade**. This is a religious war. Its aim is to take control of the holy city of Jerusalem.

1187   Muslim leader Saladin recaptures Jerusalem from the crusaders.

1184   Pope Lucius III sets up the **Holy Inquisition**. This is a group set up by the Church. Its job is to find people guilty of **heresy** (see page 53) in Italy, Spain, and France.

FURTHER READING

BOOKS

Eyewitness Guide: Castle, Christopher Gravett (Dorling Kindersley, 2002)

Eyewitness Guide: Medieval Life, Andrew Langley (Dorling Kindersley, 2002)

History in Art: The Middle Ages, Fiona MacDonald (Raintree, 2005)

Medicine in the Middle Ages, Ian Dawson (Hodder Wayland, 2005)

The Usborne Book of Castles, Leslie Sims (Usborne Publishing, 2005)

WEBSITE

• http://www.bbc.co.uk/history/british/middle_ages/ This website has many articles on different aspects of life in medieval times.

GLOSSARY

apprentice young man who is being trained in a craft or trade

baron high-ranking noble. Barons have titles such as duke or count. A baron must provide knights for the king's army in wartime.

bishop high-ranking priest. He is in charge of all the churches and priests in a large area.

Black Death deadly disease or plague. It swept through Europe in the 14th century and killed millions of people.

chivalry code of behaviour for knights

conquer take control of an area by force

craftsman person who is skilled in a trade or in making things with their hands

crusade war fought by Christians to take control of the Holy Land

fallow (of land) left without crops growing in it

famine great lack of food for a very large number of people

feudalism system in which a knight serves a lord or king in return for protection or support

guild organization of craftsmen or merchants. Each craft and trade has its own guild.

heresy crime of disagreeing with the teachings of the Church

Holy Inquisition organization set up by the medieval Church to investigate heresy

Holy Land modern-day Israel and Palestine. The land is connected with events in the Bible.

Holy Roman Empire medieval empire that was named after the ancient Roman Empire. It included Germany, Italy, Switzerland, Austria, Belgium, the Netherlands, and parts of France and eastern Europe.

humour one of four substances that medieval doctors believed circulated in the body. These are known as blood, phlegm, choler, and melancholy.

joust fighting contest between two knights on horseback

knight noble who fights in armour and on horseback

Latin language of the ancient Romans

manor village and its farmlands. A manor house is the home of the lord who owns the manor.

merchant someone who makes a living by buying and selling things

minstrel travelling musician

monastery place where a group of monks live and work

patron saint religious person who is associated with a place, country, or activity

pilgrim someone who goes on a journey to a holy place for religious reasons

pilgrimage long journey to a holy place

pope leader of the Catholic Church

rank position or level of importance

Roman Empire lands ruled by ancient Rome

serf poor farmer who lives on land owned by a lord. Serfs obey and work for the lord. They have little freedom.

tournament series of fighting contests between knights

Viking pirate or raider from northern Europe. Vikings attacked the coasts of northwestern Europe between the 8th and 11th centuries.

INDEX